W9-AVN-052

21st Century Junior Library

Citizenship

by Lucia Raatma

CHERRY LAKE PUBLISHING * ANN ARBOR, MICHIGAN

CHERRY LAKE Publishing

Published in the United States of America by Cherry Lake Publishing
Ann Arbor, Michigan
www.cherrylakepublishing.com

Content Adviser: David Wangaard, Executive Director, SEE: The School for Ethical Education, Milford, Connecticut

Reading Adviser: Marla Conn, ReadAbility, Inc.

Photo Credits: Cover, ©iStockphoto.com/asiseeit; page 4, ©Yellowind/Dreamstime.com; page 6, ©Nytumbleweeds/Dreamstime.com; page 8, ©Morgan Lane Photography/Shutterstock, Inc.; page 10, ©Rtimages/Shutterstock, Inc.; page 12, ©Darrin Henry/Shutterstock, Inc.; page 14, ©Sonya Etchison/Dreamstime.com; page 16, ©archana bhartia/Shutterstock, Inc.; page 18, ©Tetra Images/Alamy; page 20, ©iStockphoto.com/CEFutcher

LIBRARY OF CONGRESS CATALOGING-IN-PUBLICATION DATA
Raatma, Lucia.
 Citizenship/by Lucia Raatma.
   pages cm.—(Character education) (21st century junior library)
 Includes bibliographical references and index.
 ISBN 978-1-62431-154-3 (lib. bdg.)—ISBN 978-1-62431-220-5 (e-book)—
ISBN 978-1-62431-286-1 (pbk.)
 1. Citizenship—Juvenile literature. I. Title.
JF801.R32 2013
 323.6—dc23   2013004805

Cherry Lake Publishing would like to acknowledge the work of
The Partnership for 21st Century Skills.
Please visit www.p21.org for more information.

Printed in the United States of America
Corporate Graphics Inc.
July 2013
CLFA13

CONTENTS

Always throw your trash in a garbage can or a recycling bin.

What Is Citizenship?

Leslie and Cal were walking home from school one day. They were enjoying candy bars. Leslie threw her candy wrapper on the ground when she was done.

"You should pick that up," said Cal.

"Why?" asked Leslie.

"A good **citizen** doesn't throw trash on the ground," Cal answered.

Good citizens keep their yards clean so the neighborhood will look nice.

A good citizen helps make the world a better place. This means helping your family, **community**, and planet. Good citizens know their actions affect others. They try to make good choices in everything they do.

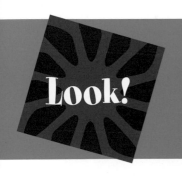

Look!

Look around your neighborhood. Do you see any ways you could help out your neighbors?

Recycling is part of being a good citizen.

Being a Good Citizen

There are many ways to be a good citizen. Peter does many chores at home. He **recycles** bottles, cans, and paper. He also cleans up after his pets. These actions show that he cares about his home and his community.

Throw away trash that you find on the ground.

You can be a good citizen by keeping your community clean and safe. Sally looks at her local streets, sidewalks, and parks. She picks up any trash she sees. She also tells an adult if she sees broken glass or other dangerous items. This won't just help one person. It will make her community better for everyone.

Create!

Sit down with your family. Make a list of the ways you can help your community. Think of things your neighbors need. Put the list in a spot where you will see it often.

Try to make new students feel welcome at your school.

You can show good citizenship by trying to make your school better. Do you see things that need fixing? Report them to the office.

Andre had a new student in his class. He wanted to make her feel welcome. Andre invited the new student to eat lunch with him and his friends. He also included her in a game at recess.

Try to stay on sidewalks instead of walking in people's yards.

You can be a good citizen in your community. One way is to obey the laws. Don't be loud or cause problems for your neighbors. Never hurt or take someone else's property.

Dave tells an adult when he sees other people breaking the law. This helps keep his community safe from crime.

Ask Questions!

Write down two rules that you must follow at home. Then ask two friends to name two rules that they must follow at home. Were any of the rules your friends named the same as your family's rules?

Newspapers can help you learn about what is going on in your community and in the world.

Spreading Citizenship

Being a good citizen means keeping up with what is happening in your community. Tracy reads newspapers and magazines to learn about **candidates** who are running for office. She isn't old enough to vote yet. But she can start learning about how leaders are elected.

A food drive is a great way to help people in need.

Many people show their good citizenship by getting involved with local **charities**. Nate and his family **volunteer** their time at a soup kitchen. Others might hold a bake sale or a raffle to make money. Find out what you can do to help. Then do your part to pitch in.

Following the rules makes the world a safer place for everyone.

Think about where you live. Show good citizenship. Do your part to make your world better. Other people **appreciate** it when you are a good citizen. Your actions may help them be good citizens, too!

Think!

Imagine that no one in your town was a good citizen. No one obeyed the laws. No one worked together or helped one another. What would it be like to live in that town?

GLOSSARY

appreciate (uh-PREE-shee-ate) to value or enjoy someone or something

candidates (KAN-duh-dates) people who are applying for a job or running in an election

charities (CHAYR-uh-teez) groups that raise money and help people in need

citizen (SIH-tuh-zun) someone who lives in a certain town or country

community (kuh-MYOO-nuh-tee) a group of people who live in the same area or who have something in common with one another

recycles (ree-SYE-kuhlz) processes old items so they can be used to make new products

volunteer (vol-uhn-TIHR) offer to do a job for no pay

FIND OUT MORE

BOOKS

Small, Mary. *Being a Good Citizen.* Minneapolis: Picture Window Books, 2006.

Suen, Anastasia. *Vote for Isaiah! A Citizenship Story.* Edina, MN: Magic Wagon, 2009.

WEB SITES

KidsHealth—Be a Volunteer
http://kidshealth.org/kid/feeling /thought/volunteering.html
Learn more about volunteering.

The Democracy Project— Inside the Voting Booth
http://pbskids.org/democracy /vote/index.html
Learn more about voting and how one person's vote can make a difference.

INDEX

ABOUT THE AUTHOR

Lucia Raatma has written dozens of books for young readers. They are about famous people, historical events, ways to stay safe, and other topics. She lives in Florida's Tampa Bay area with her husband and their two children.